Introduction

To begin with, I'll sneak in two sentences of theory:

- A time-varying magnetic field produces an electric field.
- The flowing current and alternating electric field create a magnetic field.

Now I will explain what they mean in practice.

When a wire is placed in an alternating magnetic field, a voltage is induced in it. This is beneficial as well as harmful. Beneficial, because this is how generators work (e.g. bicycle, car, power plants). In them, a winding rotates inside the magnet. From the point of view of the winding, the magnetic field in which it is located has a variable intensity and a potential difference appears at the ends of the coil winding.

The alternating magnetic field does not select. It induces a voltage in all conductors within its range. If it is an electrical device, it will disturb its operation. Therefore, people who have pacemakers cannot be treated with the magnetic field.

Every electronic circuit described in this book is a source of a magnetic field. Are they safe? Yes! They are powered by low voltage, low currents flow through them.

According to the standards in many countries, AC voltage up to 24 V is considered safe.

Can an electronics, electrician, automation engineer deal with a magnetic field that can cause damage. Yes! The source of the field can be, for example, a radio transmitter that emits electromagnetic waves not only at the nominal frequency, but also at harmonic frequencies.

Harmonic frequencies are created, for example, when the device is overdriven, when a sinusoidal waveform given to the input of the device changes into a square wave at its output.

From the point of view of the impact on other circuits, the strength of the magnetic field is important. The more violent the current flow, the stronger the field emission. Therefore, impulse devices (power supplies, converters, Tesla coils, etc.) are a source of strong electromagnetic interference. It is necessary to "de-interference", "shield".

This book is not a saboteur's manual, but it is intended to show the electronic engineer that everyday devices, if they spark (because the interference suppression capacitor has lost its capacitance) or emit a strong magnetic field (because the screen has not been closed after repair) can interfere with the operation of electroacoustic devices, computers or medical electronics.

As far as possible, experiments with electronic circuits should be carried out in a place with the least density of cables: electrical installations, overhead lines, antenna installations. The farther it is from cables, the less chance it has of interfering with or damaging your own or your neighbor's electronic equipment.

The ideal place to study electronic circuits is a Faraday cage. Its role can be played by a metal garage, the structure of which is grounded. In order for the interference not to spread over the mains, you need to organize your own power source in the form of a power generator. This solution guarantees not only: avoiding losses in electronic equipment, not interfering with devices in the vicinity, but also protection against eavesdropping. Yes! Electromagnetic waves emitted by electronic devices can be deliberately intercepted in order to obtain the information contained therein.

Emitting electromagnetic interference may be against the law. The consequences depend on the scale and motives of the action. If our antenna amplifier is aroused and makes it difficult for neighbors to watch TV - the consequences may be symbolic. If intentional damage to electronic equipment is proven - the case may have more severe consequences.

Locating the source of electromagnetic radiation is not difficult. All you need is a directional antenna with a selective amplifier and a signal level indicator.

Devices known as dirty jammers have been used to disrupt candy bar vending machines, money changers, and gaming machines. They ceased to be effective, because after the incidents noticed, the design of these devices was changed.

Chapter 1. Can the generated magnetic field affect the operation of electronic devices?

The easiest way to check this is by experience. For this purpose, I will build a circuit that detects electromagnetic radiation, but if it fails, it will not be a great loss (Figure 1.1).

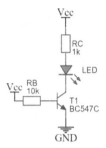

Figure 1.1. Test circuit diagram

When the circuit is turned on, the LED will be on (Figure 1.2). It will react to a weak external magnetic impulse by changing the brightness of the light. A strong impulse will damage the components and the LED will turn off.

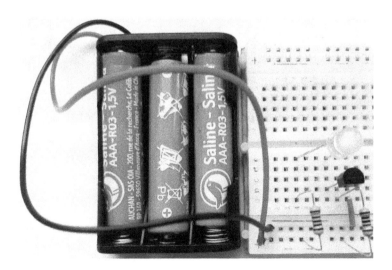

Figure 31.2. The test circuit is powered from a voltage source of approximately 4.5 V

What will be the source of the magnetic field? Coil (Figure 1.9). To make it, I will use a winding copper wire with a diameter of 0.75 mm (Figure 1.3.).

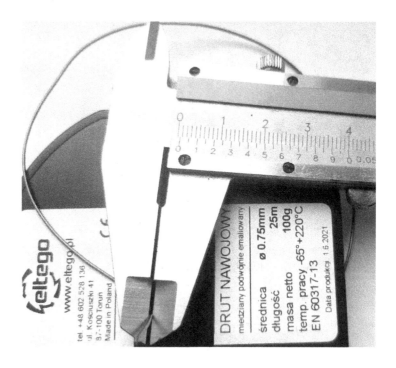

Figure 1.3. The winding wire is covered with insulating varnish

I will wind the coil on a thick felt-tip pen (Figure 1.4).

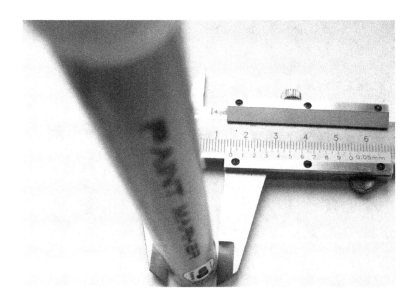

Figure 1.4. The coil will have an inside diameter of approximately 17mm. The closer the diameter of your coil is to this value, the closer the experiment results will be to those described

So that when winding the coil I did not miss the third hand, I attached one end of the wire to the felt-tip pen with insulation (Figure 1.5).

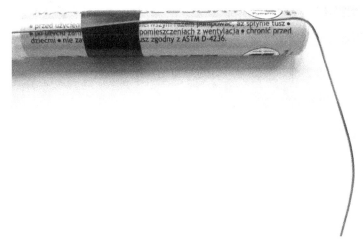

Figure 1.6 shows the coil after winding is complete.

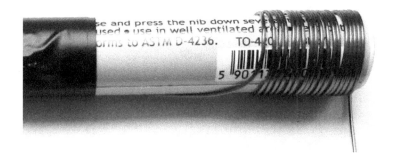

Figure 1.6. The coil has 17 turns

After winding the coil, I secured it with insulation and cut the winding wire (Figure 1.7).

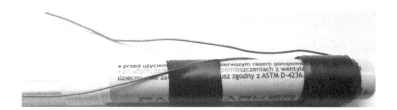

Figure 1.7. I secured the wound coils by unrolling them with several turns of insulation

The enamel covering the winding wire is insulation. So that the coil could be connected to the circuit, I cleaned the ends of the wire with a sharp tool (Figure 1.8).

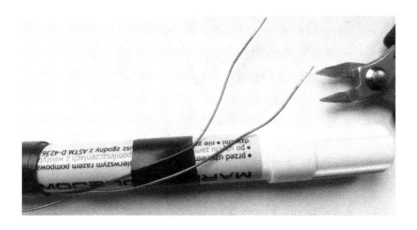

Figure 1.8. The stripped wire is lighter in color than the one that is enameled

The coil retains its shape after being removed from the felt-tip pen (Figure 1.9).

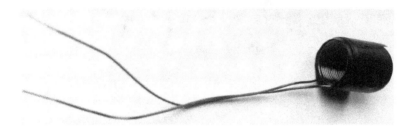

Figure 1.9. The coil

How to generate a strong magnetic field? It is necessary to cause a rapidly increasing current to flow through the conductor, which will reach a high intensity in a short time. The source from which the system will be powered can be a capacitor with a large capacity (Figure 1.10).

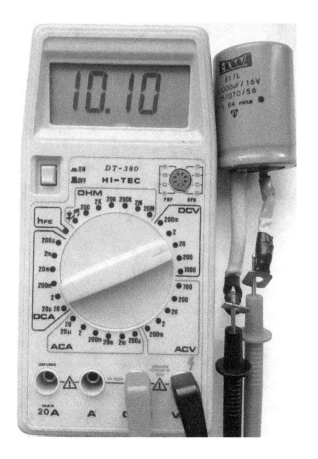

Figure 1.10. The capacitor was charged to 10.10V

*When measured with a capacitance meter,
the capacitor in Figure 1.10 has a capacitance
of 12.41 mF. Is that a lot? Such a capacitance
charged to a voltage of 10.10 V is enough to
make an LED powered by it with a 3.3 kΩ
limiting resistor connected in series shine for
3 minutes and 30 seconds.*

I placed the coil close to the test circuit (Figure 1.11). I turned on the power to the test system. The LED was on. I connected a capacitor to the coil. The LED flashed a little brighter.

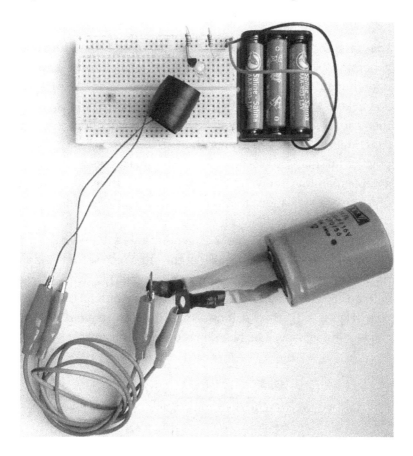

Figure 1.11. The external magnetic field did not damage the diode, but caused a temporary change in its brightness.

Chapter 2. Interference transmitter

The source of interference may be a generator built using a NAND gate made in TTL technology (Figure 2.1.).

The task of the capacitance C1 is to change the frequency generated by the circuit. Picofarads are a small value and the operation of the circuit is affected by the mounting capacitances and even the proximity of the hand to the system. The values of the capacitance contributed by the human body or the experimental plate are comparable to the capacitance C1. In practice, it may be necessary to use capacitors with a value greater than that shown in the diagrams, e.g. from 70 pF to 150 pF, to create oscillations that can be received by VHF radio.

The layout shown in Figure 2.1. generates a square wave. It is barely audible in the loudspeaker of the radio receiver. If the input of the generator (leg 9 of the integrated circuit) is given a signal with an acoustic frequency, e.g. from a generator built on the 555 chip (Figure 2.2), then a tone similar to the frequency of the modulating signal will be heard in the radio loudspeaker.

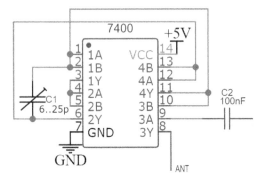

Figure 2.1. Modulated generator built using the 7400 chip in TTL technology

12

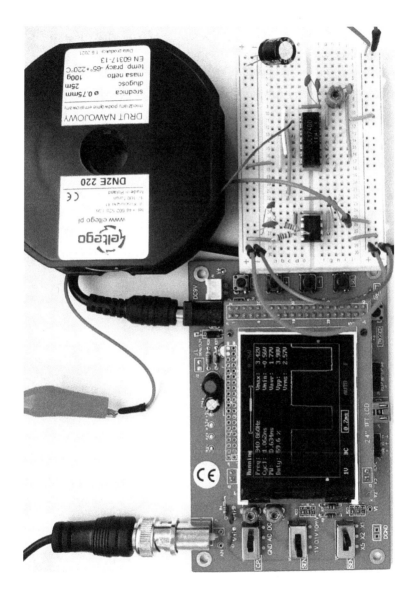

Figure 2.2. Generator built using the 7400 chip modulated with a signal coming from the 555 chip (square wave with a frequency of 940.86 Hz).

13

In my circuit, to obtain interference at a frequency of about 101 MHz, I used a capacitor C1 consisting of four elements connected in parallel: a trimmer with a capacitance of 6 pF to 30 pF and three capacitors with a value of 68 pF each.

I have shown the output signal in Figure 2.3.

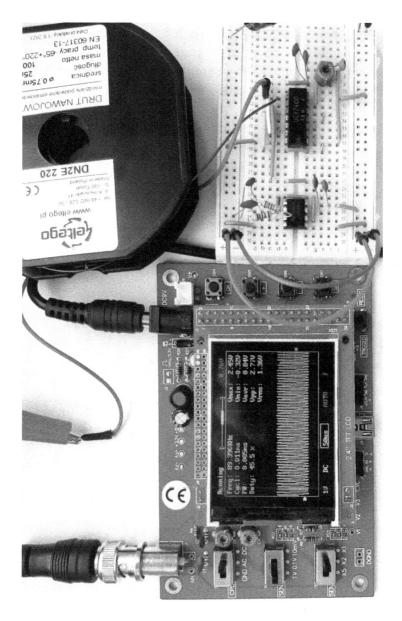

Figure 2.3. The oscilloscope shows a frequency of 89.39 kHz. It is one of the components of the output signal

I connected an "antenna" made of winding wire to the output of the generator. After unrolling it, you can bring it closer to the radio receiver, its power cord and observe the influence of the position of the antenna on the received interference.

The generator is a source of interference. Try to use it with the antenna connected as short as possible so as not to disturb the neighbors listening to the radio.

To check how the generator works, you need to set the capacitance C1 in the middle range of values. Then you need to turn on the generator. The test device is a radio receiver (can be one from a smartphone). You need to turn the volume down to about half the output power and tune the radio until you hear a whirr in the loudspeaker. To verify that we have successfully tuned the receiver to our generator, we need to turn off the power to the circuit. If the hum in the loudspeaker dies down, we have heard our own source of interference. If the volume of the sound has not changed, we have tuned in to another source of interference. In this case, change the capacitance value by turning the axis of the trimmer C1 and repeat the process of tuning the generator and the radio.

It will be easier to understand the operation of the circuit if instead of "black boxes" it is presented as gates (Figure 2.4).

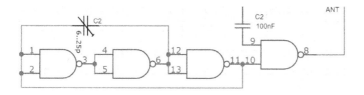

Figure 2.4. The layout in Figure 2.1. drawn with gates

The circuit uses TTL gate propagation times. The oscillation period has a value close to the sum of times Tphl + Tplh of a single gate. Therefore, interference is generated in the VHF frequency range.

> *The TTL circuit generates a square wave. In addition to the fundamental frequency, frequencies 3, 5, 7, 9, etc. times higher are emitted. The fact that the signal is received on the radio only in one place on the scale does not mean that there are no more interferences. They can enter the frequency band used by television transmitters, aviation, etc.*

The TTL gate in Figure 2.3 draws 25 mA. Combined with the voltage of 5 V, this gives a power of 125 mW. Only part of it is radiated by the antenna (provided that the antenna is impedance matched). Therefore, the range of emitted interference is small.

> *You may only use the circuit to test your designs for interference. Your neighbors will thank you if you do your experiments in a Faraday cage or far away from buildings.*

Chapter 3. Portable storm

Atmospheric discharges cause interference with radio waves at a considerable distance from the point of lightning strike. What about sparking devices: electric motors, internal combustion engines? They are also a source of interference.

A large amount of current is required to generate a spark. I will power the circuit from four series-connected batteries (Figure 3.1).

Figure 3.1. Batteries connected in series produce a voltage of 5.5 volts

The advantage of batteries is that they can draw a current of up to 5 A (Figure 3.2).

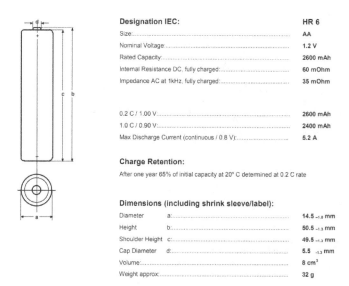

Designation IEC:		HR 6
Size:		AA
Nominal Voltage:		1.2 V
Rated Capacity:		2600 mAh
Internal Resistance DC, fully charged:		60 mOhm
Impedance AC at 1kHz, fully charged:		35 mOhm
0.2 C / 1.00 V:		2600 mAh
1.0 C / 0.90 V:		2400 mAh
Max Discharge Current (continuous / 0.8 V):		5.2 A

Charge Retention:

After one year 65% of initial capacity at 20° C determined at 0.2 C rate

Dimensions (including shrink sleeve/label):

Diameter	a:	14.5 -1.0 mm
Height	b:	50.5 -1.3 mm
Shoulder Height	c:	49.5 -1.3 mm
Cap Diameter	d:	5.5 -1.3 mm
Volume:		8 cm³
Weight approx:		32 g

Figure 3.2. Part of the Varta 5716 battery data sheet[1]

In the experiment, I will use a voltage converter available on popular auction sites. It supplies voltages up to 400 kV. To power it, use a voltage source of 3 V to 6 V, which is able to supply a current of 2 A to 5 A. Rechargeable batteries are perfect for this purpose.

Sparks will jump between the spark plug electrodes (Figure 3.3).

---

[1] Source:
https://www.multibatt.be/wa_files/Varta_20AA_202600mah_20Ni-mh_20Rechargeable.pdf; Accessed August 17, 2023.

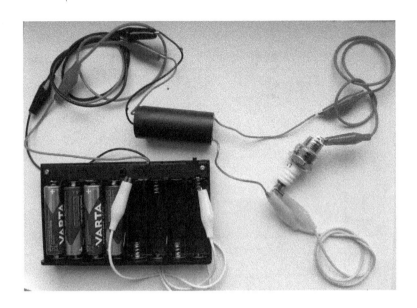

Figure 3.3. The black cylinder is the converter that powers the spark plug

*In an internal combustion engine, the
electrodes of the spark plug are inside a
metal body that limits the propagation of the
electromagnetic wave.*

Emitted interference is audible in the radio receiver.

In one of the earlier chapters, I discharged a large capacitor through a coil and checked the effect of the emitted field on the operation of an electronic circuit. I will check the effect on the transistor and the LED of the field created by discharging through the coil of the high-voltage converter (Figure 3.4). I connected a spark plug to the output of the transducer. When the voltage at the output of the converter is high enough, it causes a spark-over and a rapid current flow. The current flows through the coil. The magnetic field affects the test system. When the field emission starts, the LED diodes flicker.

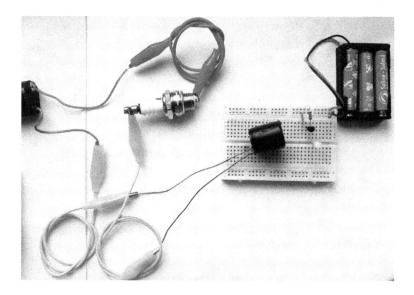

Figure 3.4. The circuit consisting of a diode and a transistor reacts to the external magnetic field by changing the brightness of the diode

The more violent the current flows through the coil, the stronger the field it will create. This can be achieved by spreading the wires between which the spark jumps over a greater distance.

I replaced the spark plug with two wires terminated with "crocodile clips" (Figure 3.5). The "crocodile clips" are attached to an insulator - a pencil. The spark jumps farther than a spark plug. The LED flashes more intensively.

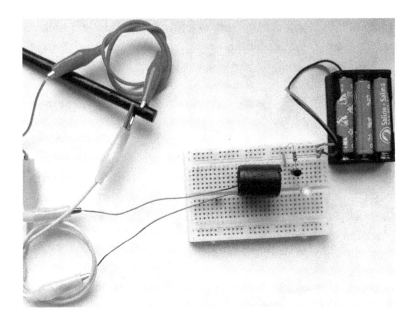

Figure 3.5. The sparks jump less often, but the current flow is more intense

The spark jumped about 3 mm (Figure 3.6).

Figure 3.6. The gap between the wires that the spark was traversing

Discrete components (transistor, LED) are much more resistant to external magnetic fields. When I made a test circuit with a 74HC00 gate, an LED and a 470 Ω resistor, it was destroyed after a few electromagnetic pulses (Figure 3.7).

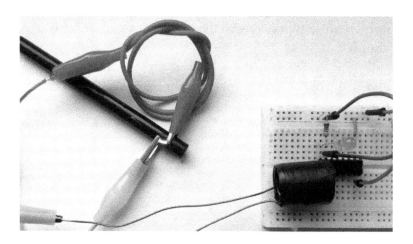

Figure 3.7. After a few pulses passed through the coil, the LED went out. The integrated circuit has been damaged

Warning !

I performed the experiments with such an intensity of the magnetic field that the effect was visible and the smartphone with which I documented the experiments was not damaged. Using higher supply voltages than I have described may create a magnetic field that will reach the equipment you did not want to disturb.

Aiming the coil at devices other than the test circuit may damage them!

Index

www.ingramcontent.com/pod-product-compliance
Lightning Source LLC
LaVergne TN
LVHW051651050326
832903LV00034B/4818